KU-755-992

100

things you should know about

PIRATES

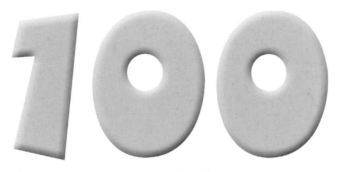

100

things you should know about

PIRATES

Andrew Langley

Consultant: Richard Tames

Miles Kelly
PUBLISHING

First published in 2004 by
Miles Kelly Publishing Ltd
Bardfield Centre, Great Bardfield, Essex, CM7 4SL

Copyright © Miles Kelly Publishing 2004

2 4 6 8 10 9 7 5 3 1

Publishing Director: Anne Marshall
Project Editor: Neil de Cort
Designer: Sally Lace
Picture Research: Liberty Newton
Proof Reading, Indexing: Lynn Bresler

All rights reserved. No part of this publication may be
reproduced, stored in a retrieval system, or transmitted by
any means, electronic, mechanical, photocopying,
recording or otherwise, without the prior permission of
the copyright holder.

Langley, Andrew

100 things you
should know
about pirates /
          J910.
          45

1559161

ISBN 1-84236-353-0

Printed in Singapore

ACKNOWLEDGEMENTS
The Publishers would like to thank the following artists who have
contributed to this book:

Chris Buzer/ Studio Galante
Peter Dennis/ Linda Rogers Assoc.
Nicholas Forder
Mike Foster/ Maltings Partnership
Terry Gabbey/ AFA
Luigi Galante/ Studio Galante
Brooks Hagan/ Studio Galante
Sally Holmes
Richard Hook/ Linden Artists Ltd

Kevin Maddison
Janos Marffy
Terry Riley
Pete Roberts/ Allied Artists
Martin Sanders
Francesco Spadoni/ Studio Galante
Rudi Vizi
Mike White/ Temple Rogers

Cartoons by Mark Davis at Mackerel

Contents

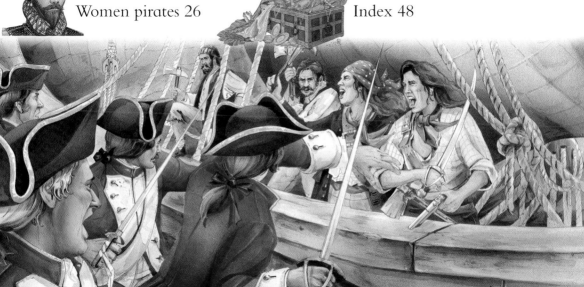

The world of pirates

1 **A pirate is a robber on the sea.** Pirates attack ships and ports, stealing treasure and other goods. As soon as the first ships began to carry cargo, pirates began to plunder them – and they are still a threat today. About 500 years ago some areas became special pirate strongholds. The 'corsairs' swooped on vessels in the Mediterranean. The 'buccaneers' of the Caribbean attacked treasure galleons on their way to Europe. The Indian Ocean and the South China Seas were also dangerous places for merchant ships to sail.

Terror from the sea

2 **The Greek islands were home to some of the earliest known pirates.** In around 500BC, there were many cargo ships trading along the Mediterranean coasts. They were easy prey for the pirates, who stole their loads of silver, copper and amber (a precious fossilized resin) before disappearing to their hideouts among the islands.

3 **In 67BC, the Roman leader Pompey sent a huge fleet to wipe out the pirates of the Mediterranean.** They had become a threat to the city of Rome itself by stealing grain supplies. For several years, the Roman campaign got rid of the pirate menace.

4 Pirates in ancient times used small, fast ships with shallow bottoms. They could steer them easily, and escape into small bays and channels where bigger boats could not go.

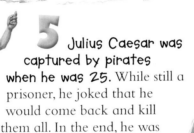

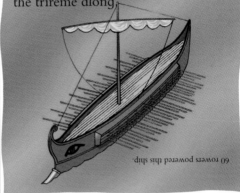

PICTURE PUZZLE

This Greek ship called a trireme was used to fight pirates. It had three banks of rowers on each side. Count them up and see how many were needed to push the trireme along.

60 rowers powered this ship.

5 Julius Caesar was captured by pirates when he was 25. While still a prisoner, he joked that he would come back and kill them all. In the end, he was released – and kept his promise. Caesar's troops seized and executed the pirates a few months later.

6 Viking ships crossed the North Sea to raid settlements on the British coast. Bands of up to 50 Vikings terrified Britons with their battle axes and wide two-edged swords. Their speedy flat-bottomed 'longships' could even carry them up rivers to attack villages inland.

Muslim marauders

7 **Pirates of the Mediterranean were known as 'corsairs'.** The most famous corsairs were Muslims from the Barbary Coast of North Africa. They took great delight in plundering Christian ships – especially when the two sides were at war after the crusades began in about 1100.

8 **The corsairs wanted people, not treasure.** They sold their ordinary captives as slaves, or forced them to work in their galleys. Richer people were more valuable. The corsairs demanded ransoms for their release.

This is a pirate blunderbuss. The wider end, or muzzle, was designed to spread the shot widely before before boarding a ship.

cannon ball

early grenade

dagger

dagger sheath

9 At the front of the ship a corsair galley had a massive ram. The galley was rammed into the side of the Christian vessel. Then soldiers called janissaries jumped aboard and quickly overpowered the enemy.

10 Corsairs fought with curved swords called scimitars. Muslim craftsmen made the sharpest and most beautiful swords and daggers in the world. Some corsairs also carried muskets, while the galleys were armed with small brass cannon.

11 The two most feared corsairs were the Barbarossa brothers. One attacked ships belonging to the Pope and even captured the town of Algiers in north Africa, but he was killed there in 1518. The other Barbarossa became an ally of the Turkish emperor.

I DON'T BELIEVE IT!

'Barbarossa' was not the brothers' real name. It was a nickname given to them by their enemies because of the colour of their beards. Barba rossa means 'Redbeard' in Latin.

11

Captured by corsairs

12 **The life of a galley slave was horrible.** The oars were so big and heavy that they needed as many as six men to pull them. The slaves were chained to rows of benches. In between the rows strode the overseer, or officer in charge. He would drive the men to work harder, either by shouting or by lashing them with his whip.

▼ Going to sea in a stolen, or even a hand-made boat, was the only way for slaves to escape.

14 **Many slaves tried to escape.** Some went inland, but found only desert regions short of food and water. The only other way was to escape by sea, making or stealing a boat. Very few got away.

13 **On land, the slaves lived in a prison, or bagnio.** Each slave had a heavy ring and chain riveted to his ankle, and was given a blanket to sleep on. When he was not rowing in the galleys, he spent his time digging or breaking rocks. There was little food apart from bread, and many slaves died in the bagnio.

15 There were Christian corsairs too. Many were based on the island of Malta, where they were supported by Christian knights on the island who wanted to see the Muslims defeated. Maltese corsairs also used galleys rowed by men captured and forced to work, and were just as brutal as their enemies in North Africa.

▼ The English and Dutch fleet bombarded Algiers with cannon to stop the corsairs and free their slaves.

QUIZ

1. Who was captured by pirates aged 25?
2. What were Viking boats called?
3. What were pirates of the Mediterranean Sea called?
4. What is a scimitar?
5. What is a bagnio?

1. Julius Caesar 2. Longships
3. Corsairs 4. A curved corsair sword
5. A prison for slaves

16 In 1816 a fleet of English and Dutch ships bombarded Algiers. They forced the corsairs to release over 3,000 slaves. A few years later French troops invaded Algiers, and brought the ravages of the corsair bands to an end.

17 Some corsairs attacked countries far from the Mediterranean. Murad Rais sailed all the way to Iceland in 1627. His plundered treasure included salted fish and leather!

The Spanish Main

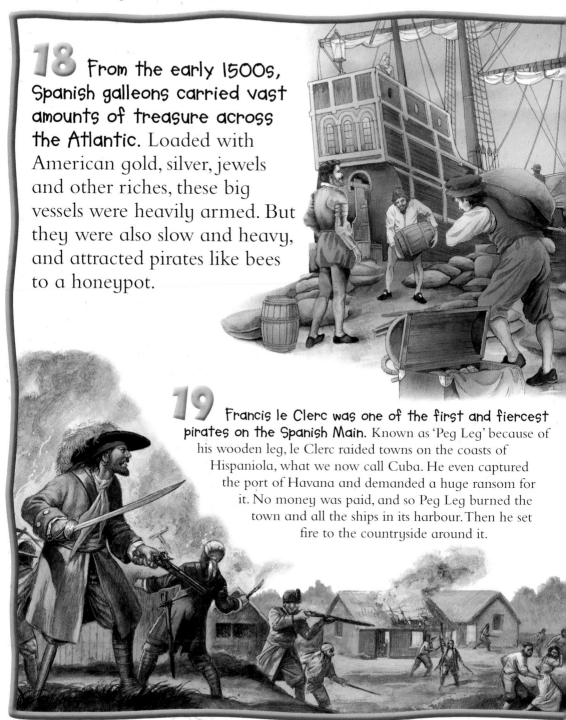

18 From the early 1500s, Spanish galleons carried vast amounts of treasure across the Atlantic. Loaded with American gold, silver, jewels and other riches, these big vessels were heavily armed. But they were also slow and heavy, and attracted pirates like bees to a honeypot.

19 Francis le Clerc was one of the first and fiercest pirates on the Spanish Main. Known as 'Peg Leg' because of his wooden leg, le Clerc raided towns on the coasts of Hispaniola, what we now call Cuba. He even captured the port of Havana and demanded a huge ransom for it. No money was paid, and so Peg Leg burned the town and all the ships in its harbour. Then he set fire to the countryside around it.

▼ The soldiers guarding the treasure were called 'conquistadores', who were the first of the Spanish soldiers to invade South America. They often travelled with the treasure ships, but were no match for the pirates.

PICTURE PUZZLE

Can you spot the different kinds of treasure hidden aboard this galleon?

You should be able to spot gold, jewels and 'pieces of eight'.

20 Soon the Spaniards began to assemble their galleons into fleets. They realised that groups of ships would be safer from pirates than single ones. Two big fleets arrived in the Spanish Main each year. One loaded up with treasure from Mexico. The other went to Panama, where it took on silver brought overland from mines in Peru, and treasures ferried across the Pacific from the Philippines. Small and heavily armed warships protected the treasure fleets as they made their way back home to Spain.

treasure ships

armed warships

▲ The treasure ships, the large ships in the middle, always sailed across the Atlantic with heavily armed warships on either side of them.

15

Sea dogs

21 John Hawkins made many raids on treasure ships in the Spanish Main. But he did not call himself a pirate. He carried a letter from his Queen, Elizabeth I of England, which allowed him to attack ships from an enemy nation. England and Spain were not at war, but they were enemies. Hawkins, and many like him, were called 'privateers'.

▲ This letter of marque was issued by King George III of England. Genuine letters contained restrictions on which ships they could attack.

▲ The slave trade lasted for hundreds of years. Up to 70,000 slaves were transported in horrible conditions every year. Some people say that a total of 15 million slaves were delivered, but many millions died on the way.

22 Hawkins' voyages made him very rich. He sailed first to West Africa where he rounded up 400 slaves and loaded them on board. Next he sailed to the Caribbean where he sold the slaves in exchange for gold, silver and pearls.

23 Walter Raleigh never found any gold in South America. He made two voyages in search of the fabulous gold-encrusted man – El Dorado. Both voyages were failures, and when he returned, Raleigh was beheaded.

24

Francis Drake was the greatest of the Elizabethan 'sea dogs'. He first went to sea at 14, and later joined his cousin John Hawkins on his expeditions. Like Hawkins, he became a privateer, and carried on an unofficial war against Spain.

▲ The route of Drake's three-year voyage round the world.

26
In 1572 Drake attacked Spanish settlements in Panama.
He ambushed a mule train laden with silver at Nombre de Dios. He became the first Englishman to see the Pacific Ocean. He vowed that one day he would sail there.

25
Drake's most amazing exploit was his voyage around the world.
He set out in 1577 and found his way to the Pacific. Here he captured the giant Spanish treasure ship 'Cacafuego', which was carrying a cargo worth over £12 million in today's money. By the time Drake got back to England in 1580, his two remaining ships were crammed with riches as well.

I DON'T BELIEVE IT!
When Drake raided the treasure store at Nombre de Dios, he landed at night, captured the guns and fought off the guards. But when the store was opened, it was empty!

Pig hunters

27 The original buccaneers were drifters and criminals on the island of Hispaniola, modern Cuba. They wandered about, hunting the wild pigs for food. They cooked them over wood fires.

28 During the 1630s, the Spanish drove out these 'buccaneers' and killed all the wild pigs. So the buccaneer bands, who had to find food somewhere, became pirates instead. They began to attack and loot passing Spanish merchant ships.

29 The first buccaneer stronghold was a small rocky island called Tortuga. It had a sheltered harbour, and was close to the main shipping route. Buccaneers built a fort at Tortuga and placed 24 cannons there, pointing out to sea.

30 Henry Morgan started out as a privateer, but soon became a famous buccaneer leader. In 1668 he led an army overland to sack the city of Portobello in Cuba. Two years later, Morgan conquered Panama City, and opened the way for pirates into the Pacific.

PICTURE PUZZLE

There are six pirate weapons hidden in this picture. Can you find a scimitar, a dagger, a pistol, a musket, an axe and a firebomb?

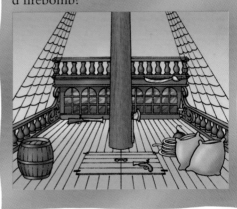

31 **The name of Francis L'Ollonais struck terror into Spanish hearts.** This buccaneer became famous for his cruel and heartless deeds. This meant that people were more likely to surrender straight away when they knew it was him.

32 **The buccaneers even invented a special kind of sword – the cutlass.** This began as a knife which they used for cutting up the wild pigs. It soon became a broad, short sword which many pirates and other sailors carried as their main weapon in battle.

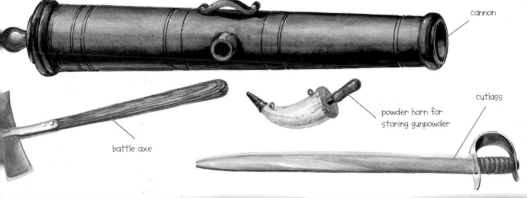

cannon

battle axe

powder horn for storing gunpowder

cutlass

Pirate stronghold

33 In the 1650s, most buccaneers moved to a new hideout on Jamaica. This was Port Royal, set at the end of a narrow spit of land. There was a fort to guard the harbour entrance, and docks where pirates could repair their ships. The British, who ruled Jamaica, did not try to interfere with the buccaneers. Port Royal was a pirate paradise!

34 Port Royal was a wild and wealthy place. The buccaneers brought their plunder to the docks to sell to merchants. With the money they roamed the streets looking for a good time. The town had 44 taverns, crowded with drunkards, pickpockets and runaway slaves as well as pirates. The money disappeared fast. One citizen wrote that the buccaneers "have been known to spend 3,000 pieces of eight [silver coins] in one night". That is £45,000 in today's money.

35 Port Royal was destroyed by a monster earthquake in 1692. Buildings collapsed, and two whole streets were swallowed up by the sea. A giant wave followed the earthquake, washing right over the town. Altogether, 4,000 people died in the disaster. Some saw it as God's punishment for their wicked ways.

QUIZ 2

1. What kind of meat did the first buccaneers eat?
2. Which island did they live on?
3. What kind of sword did the buccaneers invent?
4. Where were the treasure galleons going?
5. What were pieces of eight?

1. wild pig 2. Hispaniola 3. the cutlass 4. Spain 5. silver coins

Island of thieves

36 **Pirates had prowled the Indian Ocean for many centuries.** From bases on the Indian coast, over 100 pirate ships put to sea. They scoured the ocean all summer, seizing the cargoes of lone merchant ships.

37 **When Portuguese sailors reached the Indian Ocean, they soon became pirates too.** From about 1500, Portuguese traders began sailing from Africa to India, and then on to the Far East. They stole silks, spices, jewels and gold from the Arab merchants.

38 **The exotic treasures of the East quickly attracted many buccaneers.** They moved from the Caribbean to the Indian Ocean, many settling on the island of Madagascar. This was a wild and unexplored land, where it was easy to hide.

▲ The large island of Madagascar lies at the southeast corner of Africa. Its remote and forested coast made a perfect stronghold for pirates.

39 **William Kidd started out as a pirate-hunter, but became a pirate!** He was sent to chase pirates in the Indian Ocean in 1696. Within a few months, Kidd was attacking ordinary trading ships, including the 'Queddah Merchant' whose cargo he sold for £10,000. When he returned home he was arrested and hanged for piracy. His body was displayed in a cage at the mouth of the Thames for several years.

40 Henry Avery was feared as 'The Arch Pirate'. His most ferocious deed was the capture of the Indian Emperor's treasure ship in the Red Sea. He tortured many passengers, and terrified the women so much that they jumped overboard.

41 Kanhoji Angria was the greatest of the Indian Ocean pirates. Setting sail from India's west coast, he led his ships against any merchant ships which passed. He also built a series of forts along the coast, and defied the strength of the British navy. His followers were called 'Angrians'.

PIRATE SEARCH

The surnames of seven pirates and privateers are hidden in this letter square. Can you find them all?

B	R	N	A	D	C	X	M
D	R	A	K	E	B	N	O
L	E	C	L	E	R	C	R
K	R	K	S	E	S	W	G
L	O	I	A	A	I	G	A
D	S	D	N	L	S	G	N
C	Y	D	T	E	A	C	H

Drake, Raleigh, Morgan, Le Clerc, Read, Kidd, Teach

Junks and outriggers

42 **The South China Seas were a perfect place for pirates.** There was a maze of small islands, mangrove swamps and narrow channels to hide in, and many merchant ships to ambush. Chinese pirates became famous for their violence and brutal methods.

44 **Ching–Chi–Ling was the first great Chinese pirate leader.** With his fleet of more than 1,000 junks, he brought terror to the coast of China.

43 **Chinese pirates sailed in ships called junks.** These were often captured trading vessels, with three masts carrying square bamboo sails. The pirate captain lived in the stern cabin with his family, while his men often slept on the open deck. Junks were armed with cannon, while sailors had muskets and pistols.

▶ The Chinese had been sailing their junks for hundreds of years. A general called Zheng–he commanded ocean–going junks in the 1200s that were five times larger than European ships of the time.

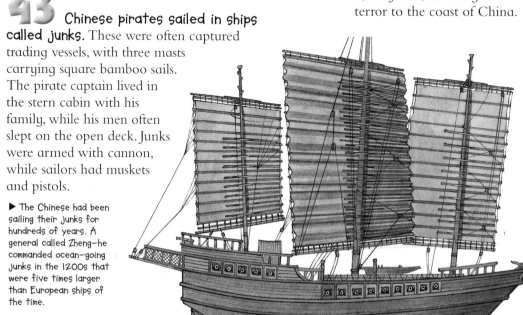

▲ With their huge fleets of pirate junks, Chinese pirates like Ching–Chi–Ling and Shap–'ng–tsai wielded huge power in the South China Sea and through to the Indian Ocean.

QUIZ 3

1. Which of these is not a type of ship?
Galleon, junk, rowlock, galley, outrigger
2. Which of these is not a type of pirate weapon?
Musket, ball valve, cutlass, sumpitan, parang
3. Where did the Balanini pirates come from?

1. rowlock 2. ball valve 3. the islands of Sulu

45 The Balanini pirates came from the islands of Sulu. They sailed in small, speedy canoes with extra beams called outriggers. In these, the Balanini swooped down on the nearby islands, kidnapping hundreds of slaves to sell in the mainland markets.

46 British ships were sent to wipe out the last great pirate fleet in 1849. They chased the junks, commanded by Shap-'ng-tsai, for over 1,000 miles before they caught them. Then they blew the junks to pieces and killed over 1,800 pirates. Shap-'ng-tsai escaped and lived to a ripe old age, but the pirate menace was ended – for the time being.

47 South Seas pirates used many fearsome weapons. They shot poisoned arrows through a blowpipe called a sumpitan. They brandished a razor-sharp chopping sword called a parang, or a knife called a kris. Some knives were completely straight, others had a rippled effect. Some were straight near the handle, or hilt, but were curved at the end. Some weapons were decorated with tufts of human hair.

◀ A kris, or 'flashing blade', used by pirates from Borneo, with its wooden scabbard.

25

Women pirates

48 **Mary Read dressed in man's clothes so that she could become a sailor.** But her ship was captured by pirates on its way to the West Indies, and Mary was taken prisoner. She joined the pirates, and then became a privateer. Once again, her ship fell victim to rival sea robbers, this time to 'Calico Jack' Rackham and his wife Anne Bonny. The two women were soon close friends. In a battle against the British navy, they both fought like demons while the rest of the crew (all men) hid below!

▶ When Grace O'Malley was pardoned for her piracy, she didn't exactly give up altogether. She just handed her business over to her sons who carried it on!

49 **Grace O'Malley commanded a pirate fleet on Ireland's west coast.** She went to sea as a young girl, and later moved into a massive stone castle right on the coast. Her fleet of twenty sailing ships and rowing boats attacked passing merchant vessels. In 1593 Grace gave up her piratical ways and begged Queen Elizabeth for a pardon. She lived to be over 70 years old.

I DON'T BELIEVE IT!

While she was a pirate Grace O'Malley cut her hair short to look like her sailors. This earned her the nickname of 'Baldy'!

50 One of the greatest woman pirates was Ching Shih.

When her husband died in 1807, she took over his raiding fleet on the Chinese coast. She was a brilliant leader, and forced her sailors to obey a strict set of rules. But life on her pirate junks was not pleasant. One captive recalled "we lived three weeks on caterpillars boiled in rice".

All aboard!

51 **Most pirate ships had to be small and fast.** On the Spanish Main, many were 'schooners', with two masts, and many were galleys with three masts like this one. The captain's cabin was in the stern, while the crew slept in the middle of the ship. Treasure, gunpowder and food stores were kept in the hold.

mizzen topsail   main topsail   mainsail   fore topsail   foresail

stern (back)

sail locker

water and stores

oars

bow (front)

bowsprit

53 **Food was mostly horrid on board a pirate ship.** The cook was often a pirate who had lost a leg or arm and couldn't do anything else. And he seldom had anything to serve except dry biscuits and pickled meat. Whenever the crew landed on a remote island, they hunted for fresh meat and – even more important – fresh water.

52 **Below decks, it was very cramped and smelly.** There was little space for the crew to sleep. Pirates barely had room to put up their hammocks, and spent most of their lives on deck, except in the worst weather.

54 **In calm weather, there was little for the pirates to do.** They would mend ropes and sails, or gamble with dice. In bad weather, or when they were chasing another ship, life was very busy. The crew might have to climb aloft in the rigging to alter the sails, keep lookout from high on the mainmast, or prepare the cannon for firing.

55 **The hull of the ship had to be kept clean.** Weeds and barnacles would slow it down, so pirates regularly dragged their vessel up onto a beach where they could scrape off any rubbish. This was also a chance to go hunting for food.

DRESS UP AS A PIRATE

Tie a red scarf round your head. Put on trousers, shirt and waistcoat – as brightly coloured as you can find. Earrings are easy, and it's not hard to make your own black moustache (out of wool) and eyepatch (cardboard and elastic bands). Now all you need is a bloodcurdling pirate yell!

56 **Most pirates dressed just like other sailors of the time.** They wore short blue jackets, checked shirts and baggy canvas trousers. But some showed off the finery they had stolen, such as velvet trousers, black felt hats, silk shirts and crimson waistcoats with gold buttons and gold lace.

▶ If a pirate had stolen clothing, they would often just sell it. But if they liked something, they may just wear it!

Attack!

57 When a pirate captain decided to attack, he raised a special flag. Not every pirate flag was the famous skull-and-crossbones. Nor were they always black. Most early pirates used a bright red flag to frighten their victims. Black flags

became popular in the early 1700s, with pirates adding their own initials or symbols.

58 Pirates depended on speed to catch their prey. If they had cannon, they would try and hit the other ship's mast or rigging. Otherwise, they fired muskets at the helmsman and other men working in the sails. In this way they could slow the ship down. If they got near enough, they might even jam the rudder so that it would not steer properly.

59 A pirate bristled with weapons. His cutlass was in his hand, and a dagger was in his belt. He might carry as many as six loaded pistols tied to a sash which he wore over his shoulder.

60 When they were near enough the attackers threw ropes with hooked grappling irons into the rigging. The ship was caught – just like a fish. The pirates climbed up the sides and jumped aboard. Sometimes they had a bloody fight on their hands. But often the enemy crew were so terrified that they surrendered straight away.

You can have your very own personal pirate flag. On a black background, draw your own scary design using bones, skulls and anything else you fancy. No-one else is allowed to copy it!

61 **Merchants often hid their cargo.** The pirates had to search everywhere and tear apart walls and doors to find it. They might even torture their captives until they told them where the treasure was.

62 **Bartholomew Roberts was probably the most successful pirate ever.** Known as Black Bart, he captured as many as 400 ships in the 1720s. Handsome, bold, he was everyone's ideal buccaneer. Yet he never drank anything stronger than tea!

◄ One of the best ways to slow a ship was to fire at the sails and rigging.

Pirate plunder

63 **All pirates dreamed of gold and silver.** Some were lucky enough to capture ships packed with them – in the form of coins, gold bars or finely made ornaments. But most merchant ships carried humbler goods, such as cloth, coal or iron.

▲ After capturing a cargo vessel, the pirates transfer all the treasure and other valuables to their own ship.

64 **The most famous coins of the Spanish Main were 'pieces of eight' or simply pesos.** These were silver, and as big as a 50 pence piece. Each one was worth about £15 in today's money.

65 **Silk and porcelain were the most precious goods from China.** For centuries, no-one in Europe knew how silk or porcelain (fine earthenware) were made. They were very delicate, and pirates had to handle them carefully.

66 **People too could be valuable.**
Pirates might hold a rich captive and
demand a ransom from their relatives.
When this was paid, the prisoner was freed.

67 **Some treasure chests were
full of jewels.** There were diamonds
from Africa, rubies and sapphires from
Burma, emeralds from Colombia and
pearls from the Persian Gulf. Many of
these were made up into beautiful jewellery.

I DON'T BELIEVE IT!

One of the most valuable cargoes
of all were the spices from India
and Sri Lanka. But they were
difficult to sell, and pirates simply
dumped them
overboard. One
beach was said to
be ankle deep in
precious spices.

68 **Pirates also needed
everyday things.** If they had been away
from land for several weeks, they would
be glad to steal food, drink and
other provisions. And fresh
guns, cannon balls and
gunpowder
always came
in useful!

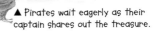

▲ Pirates wait eagerly as their
captain shares out the treasure.

69 **The captain shared out the
loot among his crew.** He did this very
carefully, so that no-one could complain.
All the same, officers got more than the
men, and the carpenter and cook got less
– because they didn't fight.

Buried treasure

70 **Pirates often hid their treasure by burying it in a remote spot.** Then they could come back and dig it up when times were quieter. After his attack on a mule train in Panama, Francis Drake found that his ship had sailed out of sight. He ordered his men to bury the looted gold and silver. Then he made a raft, paddled out to find his ships, and brought them back. That night, his men dug up the treasure and put it on board.

71 Many believe that William Kidd buried a vast store of treasure before he was captured. His piracy had gained him a huge amount of cargo, most of which he sold off or gave to his crew. But when he was arrested in 1699 he claimed that he had hidden £100,000 of treasure. Since then, hundreds of people have looked for it all over the world – but none has found a single coin.

BURIED TREASURE

Can you follow the trail and find the buried treasure?

Start on a crescent shape of sand. Go two squares northwest. Go three squares east. Follow the river right to the sea. Now go one square north, and two squares east. Finally, go two squares due north and get sight of the treasure!

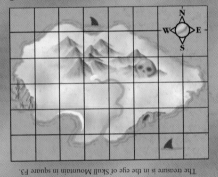

The treasure is in the eye of Skull Mountain in square F3.

▶ Pirates lived in a rough and dangerous world. There was no code of conduct between ships, so there was no reason for a pirate ship not to steal the treasure from another pirate ship!

72 The pirates of the ship 'Mary Dear' buried their loot in the Cocos Islands of the Pacific in 1820. It included over 12,000 gemstones and 9,000 gold coins, as well as seven chests of gold ornaments. Then the pirates set the ship on fire and rowed off in the longboats. When they reached land, they were arrested. None of the pirates ever went back to dig up the treasure, and no-one has discovered it since!

Desert islands

73 Some pirate captains had strict rules. 'Black Bart' Roberts made his crew promise to keep to a code of conduct. They must not gamble or fight on board ship, or keep lights and candles burning after 8 o'clock at night. Anyone who brought a woman on board, or who deserted the ship, would be put to death or marooned.

74 Marooning was a terrible fate. The pirate was left alone on a deserted island while his friends sailed away. He was given a few vital things – a pistol and ammunition, and a bottle of water. But it was almost impossible to escape, and food was hard to find. The only hope was to be picked up by another ship.

Selkirk's island was called Más á Tierra.

Goat Rock

NORTH AMERICA

ASIA

SOUTH AMERICA

AFRICA

• Más á Tierra

Goat Quarters

Open Bay

Sharpes Bay

Windy Bay

Sugar Loaf Key

77 The most famous of all castaways was Alexander Selkirk.

He was stranded on a desert island off the coast of Chile in 1704, and stayed there for five years. Selkirk was very lucky, for his island had plenty of fresh water, along with wild pigs and goats. At last, dressed in goat skins, he was rescued by a passing English ship. Writer Daniel Defoe based his story of 'Robinson Crusoe' on Selkirk's adventures.

◄ The group of islands on which Selkirk was marooned were the Juan Fernandez islands. He was very lucky that he had plenty of food and water.

75 The Pacific and the Caribbean were dotted with thousands of small islands. Very few had people living on them. Many were far away from the main shipping routes. The castaway had to hunt for fruit and small animals, or fish in the warm seas.

76 Sometimes the crew marooned their captain. This happened to Jeremy Rendell in 1684. After an argument with his crew, he was left on an island near Honduras with three other men, a gun, a canoe and a net for catching turtles. They were never heard from again.

PICTURE PUZZLE

You've been marooned on a desert island. Somewhere are hidden a water bottle, a pistol, a knife, a blanket, a kettle and an axe. Can you find them?

Storm and shipwreck

78 **Shipwreck was a pirate's biggest nightmare.** Violent storms could spring up suddenly, especially in the warm seas of the Caribbean. In 1712, a hurricane brought racing winds and giant waves into Port Royal harbour in Jamaica, smashing 38 ships.

79 **Storms could drive helpless ships onto a rocky shore.** In 1717 the pirate ship 'Whydah' was heading for Cape Cod, off North America, loaded with booty. A storm sprang up, pushing the vessel onto rocks. The mainmast fell down, and the 'Whydah' started to break up. Only two of the crew reached land alive.

81 **A hole in the hull had to be patched – fast!** The quickest way was to 'fother' it, by lowering a sail with ropes so that it fitted over the hole. But sails were not very watertight, and the patch did not last long.

80 **There were few ways to cope with an emergency.** If the ship was leaking, sailors could try pumping out the water. If the ship ran aground, they could throw heavy objects overboard, such as cannon or food barrels. This made the ship lighter, and ride higher in the water.

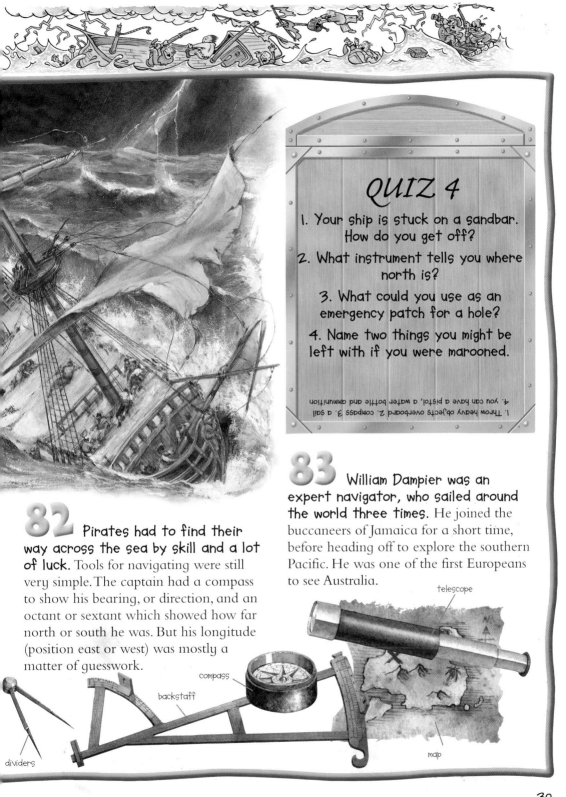

QUIZ 4

1. Your ship is stuck on a sandbar. How do you get off?

2. What instrument tells you where north is?

3. What could you use as an emergency patch for a hole?

4. Name two things you might be left with if you were marooned.

1. Throw heavy objects overboard 2. compass 3. a sail 4. you can have a pistol, a water bottle and ammunition

82 Pirates had to find their way across the sea by skill and a lot of luck. Tools for navigating were still very simple. The captain had a compass to show his bearing, or direction, and an octant or sextant which showed how far north or south he was. But his longitude (position east or west) was mostly a matter of guesswork.

83 William Dampier was an expert navigator, who sailed around the world three times. He joined the buccaneers of Jamaica for a short time, before heading off to explore the southern Pacific. He was one of the first Europeans to see Australia.

telescope

compass

backstaff

dividers

map

Hunting the pirates

84 European countries began to build bigger and stronger navies. With these, they were able to begin sweeping the pirates from the seas. Well-armed navy fleets patrolled the trouble spots. Pirates were offered free pardons if they gave up their lives of crime. Large rewards were given to anyone who helped to capture pirate ships.

85 **Edward Teach was the most terrifying pirate on the high seas.** Better known as 'Blackbeard', he made himself look as frightening as possible. He plaited ribbons into his long beard, carried six pistols slung over his shoulder, and stuck lighted matches under his hat. But one man was not afraid of Blackbeard – naval officer Robert Maynard. In 1718 he cornered the pirate, who shouted "Damnation seize my soul if I give you quarter!" Maynard leapt aboard his ship and fought him to the death. Then he cut off Blackbeard's hairy head and hung it in the bows of his vessel.

PICTURE PUZZLE

Which pirate names do these pictures make you think of?

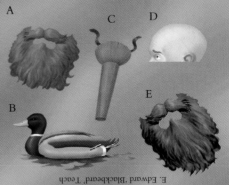

A. Barbarossa ('red beard') brothers B. Francis Drake C. Francois 'Peg-leg' Le Clere D. Grace 'Baldy' O'Malley E. Edward 'Blackbeard' Teach

86 **Steam power spelled the end for most pirates.** The navy built steam ships, which could travel much faster than the old sailing ships and did not depend on the wind. The pirates simply couldn't get away!

41

On the gallows

87 **Many captured pirates were taken back to Britain in chains.** But most never got that far. They were taken to the nearest American port and executed as quickly as possible. Only the younger criminals of 15 or 16 years old were pardoned and released.

▲ Captured prisoners were manacled together with long chains on the voyage to prison and trial.

88 **Trials in Britain lasted only one or two days.** The judges were keen to condemn the pirates as quickly as possible, so that they would frighten those still at large. Anyone who was known to have fired a cannon, carried a gun or taken part in looting was found guilty.

89 **Before and after trial, the pirates were kept in prison.** In London, this would probably be the hated Newgate Prison, which was foul-smelling, dirty and overcrowded. Many prisoners died of disease or starvation before they ever came to be executed.

▲ Newgate Prison in London was a brutal, unhealthy place.

◀ This is one of the dreaded 'hulks'. These were naval ships that had got too old to be used for sailing, so were converted and used as floating prisons for the worst criminals.

91 **The bodies were left on the gallows until the tide came in and covered them.** After three tides, it was either taken down and buried or left hanging in chains as a lesson for others. Some bodies were coated in tar so that they would last longer.

I DON'T BELIEVE IT!

After William Duell was hanged his body was taken down and washed. Then someone saw that he was still breathing! The courts did not have the heart to hang him again, so he was sent to Australia instead.

90 **Pirates that had been found guilty were hanged at Execution Dock in London.** They sometimes took a long time to die. William Kidd had to be hanged a second time after the rope broke. As a deterrent, a warning to other people who might become pirates, their bodies were displayed in cages.

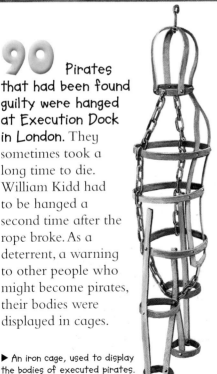

▶ An iron cage, used to display the bodies of executed pirates.

92 **The British navy destroyed many pirate ships.** An entire fleet of Chinese junks was sunk or set on fire near Hong Kong in 1849, and 400 pirates killed. The naval commander went on to smash up the pirate dockyards and confiscate all the weapons.

Pirates today

93 **Pirates are not a thing of the past.** There are still plenty of pirates operating on the seas today, especially in the Caribbean and the Far East. In 1992, there were more than 90 attacks on ships in just one part of the world – the narrow Straits of Malacca between Singapore and Sumatra. The modern day pirates move in at dead of night in small boats, and climb up ropes or bamboo poles onto the decks of the merchant ships. Within a few minutes they have stolen all the valuables on board, slipped over the side again and disappeared into the dark.

▶ Modern pirates work in a very different way to the pirates from years ago. They prefer to use stealth. This means that they do not climb onto a ship yelling and letting off fireworks as Blackbeard would have done. They prefer to sneak quietly onto a ship take what they want and leave with as little fuss as possible.

94 **Modern pirates use modern weapons.** They use machine guns, automatic rifles and speed boats. They plan their attacks with radios and computers.

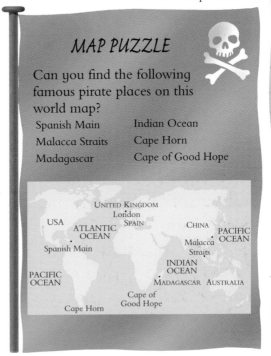

MAP PUZZLE

Can you find the following famous pirate places on this world map?

Spanish Main   Indian Ocean

Malacca Straits   Cape Horn

Madagascar   Cape of Good Hope

UNITED KINGDOM
London
USA
SPAIN
ATLANTIC
OCEAN
CHINA
PACIFIC
OCEAN
Spanish Main
Malacca
Straits
INDIAN
OCEAN
PACIFIC
OCEAN
MADAGASCAR AUSTRALIA
Cape of
Good Hope
Cape Horn

95 **People are still searching for pirate treasure.** One of the most mysterious sites is Oak Island, off the North American coast. Treasure hunters have been digging here since 1795, when three boys began to dig a pit and found a wooden platform. Was this the place where Captain Kidd or other pirates buried their plunder? Since then, diggers have gone down over 100 metres into the ground, but not a single coin has been found.

Myth and reality

▲ A scene from Robert Louis Stevenson's 'Treasure Island'. You can see Long John Silver with his parrot, the wild castaway Ben Gunn, and, of course, the treasure!

96 The best-known pirate of all is in a story book – Long John Silver. Robert Louis Stevenson's 'Treasure Island' is one of the most exciting and best-loved of all adventure stories. With its one-legged villain (Silver), its crazy castaway (Ben Gunn) and its buried treasure, this has thrilled countless readers since it first appeared in 1883. 'Treasure Island' has also been made into several films.

▲ Robert Louis Stevenson

97 Another famous make–believe pirate is Captain Hook. This nasty character appears in J.M.Barrie's fantasy 'Peter Pan'. One of his hands has been cut off by the hero Peter Pan and fed to a crocodile, so the Captain has a hook instead. The play of 'Peter Pan' is staged every Christmas in London.

98 Many of us get our ideas of pirates from watching films. Ever since cinema began, pirate films have been popular. Great actors have starred in them, from Douglas Fairbanks and Errol Flynn to Dustin Hoffman and Mel Gibson. But these films usually show a very romantic and fun-filled picture of pirate life, and leave out most of the pain and savagery.

99 **There are cartoon pirates too.** Many picture books feature jolly pirates who are not frightening at all! The best-known of these is Captain Pugwash, who is not just stupid, but cowardly as well. Only his cabin boy Tom saves him from complete disaster at the hands of his arch-enemy, Cut-throat Jake.

I DON'T BELIEVE IT!

The story of the dreaded Blackbeard was actually put on stage in 1798 – as a ballet!

◀ Real pirates were never as kind-hearted as the jolly 'Pirates of Penzance'.

100 **The most unlikely pirates of all appear on the stage in an operetta.** 'The Pirates of Penzance', created by Gilbert and Sullivan, are real softies who refuse to rob orphans. Needless to say, all their victims claim to be orphans!

Index

The Colours
We Eat

KU-755-999

Red Foods

Patricia Whitehouse

A L I S

1669546

www.raintreepublishers.co.uk
Visit our website to find out more information about **Raintree** books.

To order:
 Phone 44 (0) 1865 888112
 Send a fax to 44 (0) 1865 314091
Visit the Raintree Bookshop at **www.raintreepublishers.co.uk** to browse our catalogue and order online.

First published in Great Britain by Raintree, Halley Court, Jordan Hill, Oxford OX2 8EJ, part of Harcourt Education.
Raintree is a registered trademark of Harcourt Education Ltd.

© Harcourt Education Ltd 2003
The moral right of the proprietor has been asserted.

All rights reserved. No part of this publication may be reproduced, stored in a retrieval system, or transmitted in any form or by any means, electronic, mechanical, photocopying, recording, or otherwise, without either the prior written permission of the publishers or a licence permitting restricted copying in the United Kingdom issued by the Copyright Licensing Agency Ltd, 90 Tottenham Court Road, London W1T 4LP (www.cla.co.uk).

Editorial: Nick Hunter and Diyan Leake
Design: Sue Emerson (HL-US) and Joanna Sapwell (www.tipani.co.uk)
Picture Research: Amor Montes de Oca (HL-US) and Maria Joannou
Production: Jonathan Smith

Originated by Dot Gradations
Printed and bound in China by South China Printing Company

ISBN 1 844 21606 3 (hardback)
07 06 05 04 03
10 9 8 7 6 5 4 3 2 1

ISBN 1 844 21613 6 (paperback)
07 06 05 04 03
10 9 8 7 6 5 4 3 2 1

British Library Cataloguing in Publication Data
Whitehouse, Patricia
Red Foods
641.3
A full catalogue record for this book is available from the British Library.

Acknowledgements
The publishers would like to thank the following for permission to reproduce photographs: Amor Montes de Oca p. 23 (stone); Craig Mitchelldyer Photography pp. 20L, 20R, 21; Dwight Kuhn pp. 10, 15, back cover (strawberry); Fraser Photos (Greg Beck) pp. 1, 5, 6, 17, 22, 23 (sauce), 24; Heinemann Library (Michael Brosilow) pp. 4, 7, 12, 16, 18, 19, 23 (jam, peel, seed); Rick Wetherbee p. 8; Visuals Unlimited pp. 9 (Wally Eberhart), 13 (D. Cavagnaro), 14 (D. Cavagnaro), back cover (pepper, D. Cavagnaro).

Cover photograph of fruit and vegetables, reproduced with permission of Heinemann Library (Michael Brosilow).

ABERDEENSHIRE LIBRARY AND INFORMATION SERVICE	
1669546	
CAW	335705
J641.3	£4.99
JU	PORP

 CAUTION: Children should be supervised by an adult when handling food and kitchen utensils.

Some words are shown in bold, **like this.** You can find them in the glossary on page 23.

Contents

Have you eaten red foods?

Colours are all around you.

How many different colours can you see in these foods?

All of these foods are red.

Which ones have you eaten?

What are some red fruits?

Some apples are red.

The red part of an apple is called the **peel**.

seeds

Pomegranates are red fruit.

They have lots of **seeds** inside them.

What are some red vegetables?

Some cabbages are red.

We can cook them or put them in **salads**.

This onion is red.

The part of the onion that we eat is under the red skin.

Have you tried these red fruits?

Strawberries are red and sweet.

They are tasty and good for you!

stone

Cherries are good for you, too.

Watch out for the **stones** inside them!

Have you tried these red vegetables?

Kidney beans are small and red.

Make sure you cook them first, to make them soft.

These potatoes have red skins.

Did you know you can leave the skins on when you cook potatoes?

Have you tried these hot red foods?

Chilli peppers taste hot.

People use them in spicy dishes.

Red radishes are hot and crunchy.

They are tasty in **salads**.

Have you tried these soft red foods?

Strawberry **jam** is a soft red food.

Try eating it on bread or toast.

Tomato **sauce** is made by cooking tomatoes until they are soft.

It's yummy!

What drinks and soups are red?

Cranberry juice is made by squeezing the juice out of cranberries.

It's tasty and good for you!

Have you eaten beetroot soup?

The colour of the beetroot makes the soup red!

Recipe: Healthy Red Fruit Salad

❗ Ask an adult to help you.

First, wash some strawberries, cherries and raspberries.

Take out the cherry **stones**.

Next, mix all the fruit in a bowl.

Now eat your healthy red
fruit salad!

Yum!

Quiz

Can you name these red foods?

Look for the answers on page 24.

Glossary

jam
a sweet food made from fruit.
It is put on bread.

peel
skin that covers a fruit
or vegetable

sauce
a thick food that is eaten with
other food

seed
the part of a plant that grows
into another plant

salad
a cold dish made up of chopped
fruit or vegetables

stone
one hard seed inside a fruit

Index

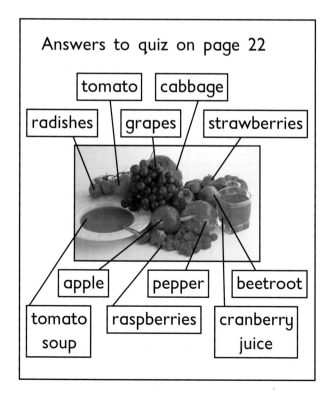

Answers to quiz on page 22

tomato   cabbage

radishes   grapes   strawberries

apple   pepper   beetroot

tomato soup   raspberries   cranberry juice

24